FIVE DECADES
UK Bhangra Pioneer since 1964

Balbir Bhujhangy

Satty Bilan

Grosvenor House
Publishing Limited

This book is published by
Grosvenor House Publishing Ltd
Link House
140 The Broadway, Tolworth, Surrey, KT6 7HT.
www.grosvenorhousepublishing.co.uk

A CIP record for this book
is available from the British Library

ISBN 978-1-80381-196-3
eBook ISBN 978-1-80381-197-0

About the Editor

I am the eldest daughter of Balbir Bhujhangy, Satty Bilan. I am not a professional writer or editor but wanted to help my dad write the main chapters of his life. This biography is not meant to be an extensive review of his life even though my father had many interesting stories about the music industry, his fellow musicians, his family members as well as those that betrayed him during his journey. We have kept it brief on purpose, but we may expand on certain chapters in the near future.

Thank you all for the support you have given my father for the past 55 years, he is a very kind and humble man who is passionate about his music and very professional. I wish him a long, healthy and happy life. He is our best friend!

Please submit any feedback or comments to:
Email: info@bhujhangy.com

Dedication

I dedicate this book to my wife, our children, and our grandchildren. I hope to pass on my legacy, hard work and determination to future generations. I would also like to thank my wife, Amarjit Kaur, for all her love and support throughout our 40+ years together.

My life in the UK started with my elder brother, Dalbir Singh, who passed away in 2008. He was my best friend, my singing partner and my everything. He would have been very proud of this book and would have had many memories to share. My eldest brother Gurdeep Singh, recently passed away in 2021, he was my rock, was always so happy and proud of the songs I released, he will be missed dearly.

Balbir Singh Khanpur Bhujhangy
Started singing in the UK in 1964
Lead singer & owner of Bhujhangy Group since 1967

Trademark copyright

Bhujhangy TM® is registered to Balbir Singh as a Trademark; it is proven that Balbir has used this name as a performer for the past 50 years continuously.

The following trade mark violations are cited in the Trade Marks Act 1994:

- An unauthorized third party utilizes a mark that is identical to a registered trademark.
- creating confusion as to the origin of the goods or services
- Unauthorized third party uses an identical or similar trade mark on goods or services, benefitting from the reputation and operating to the detriment of the registered trade mark's character.

Balbir & Brother Gurdeep

Balbir & Brother Dalbir

Balbir Singh Khanpur
Guinness World Records

We are pleased and honoured to announce Balbir Bhujhangy, 'Bhujhangy Group UK' has been entered into the 2021 edition of the Guinness Book of World Records for 'Continuously performing as Bhujhangy, longest running band in the UK, for the past 54 years'.

A big thank you to the 350+ musicians that have played with Balbir Bhujhangy for the past 54 years as part of the Bhujhangy family.

Balbir has continuously sang as Bhujhangy for the past 54 years, 41 of those years were with his dear brother who sadly passed away in 2008.

Balbir has been rewarded for his continuous hard work and commitment to the Bhangra Industry, including his vast portfolio of charity work.

Balbir Bhujhangy still continues to perform and promote Bhangra in and outside of the UK to this day and is the only active remaining member of Bhujhangy Group.

www.bhujhangy.com

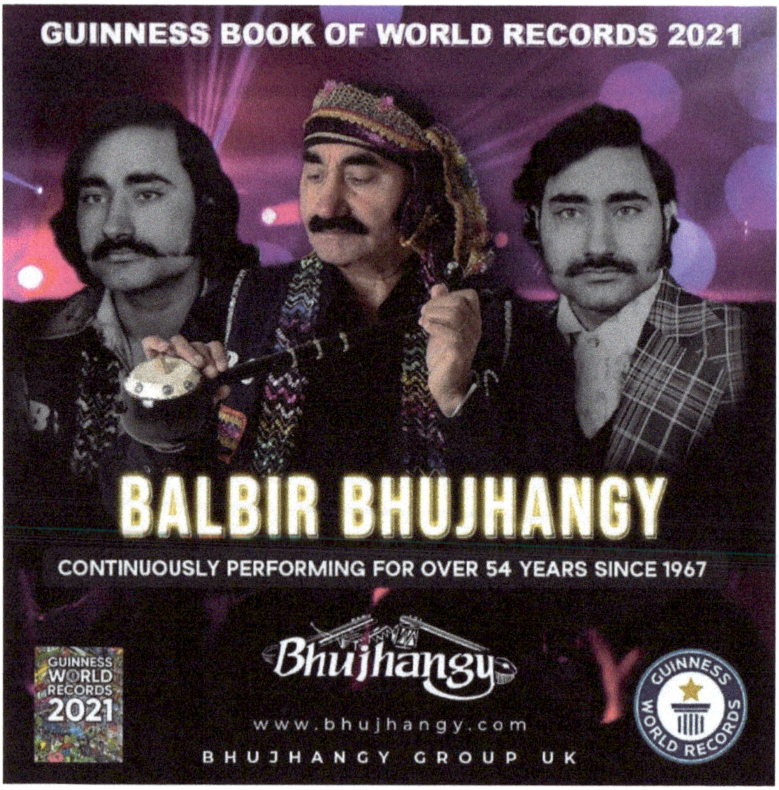

Bhujhangy™ *& Bhujhangy Group*™ *are copyright and trademark names registered by the Intellectual Property Office under Balbir Singh*

Balbir Singh has been singing and performing every year since 1964 in the UK. The name of the group, 'Bhujhangy Group', was established in 1967. Balbir has been performing the longest under the Bhujhangy name, continuously, every year for 54 years, with documented evidence and honoured by the Guinness Book of World Records in 2001, 2005, 2011, 2019 and 2021 for his continuation.

2001 & 2005

2011 & 2019

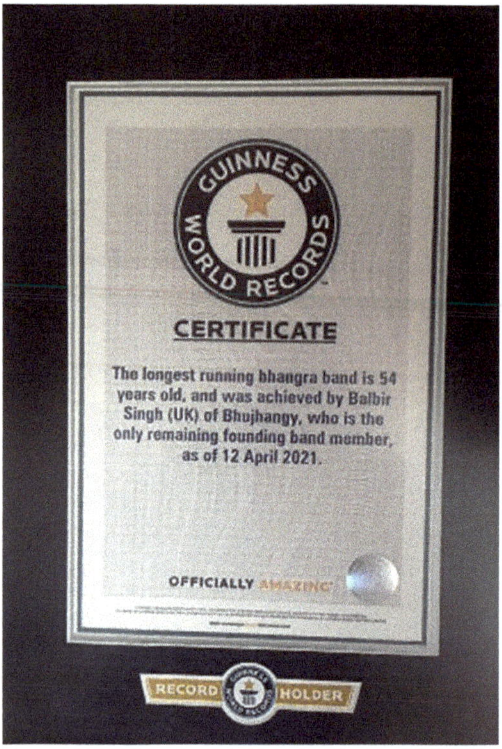

2021 – awarded as being the only member performing continuously as Bhujhangy for 54 years

Table of Contents

1947–1949 – The struggle in India

The struggle started in 1947 during the Partition of India. My grandparents were forced to leave their home, their possessions and their land at very short notice. For a lot of our grandparents, this was a familiar story.

There was a sense of fear in my father's voice whenever he spoke about the past. It seemed to be a scary memory for him. He told us the stories in short bursts but didn't go into too much detail, but our mother would go into some detail explaining how her family escaped the villages.

My father lived in West Panjab (now known as Pakistan). We had a lot of land and were fairly rich with a good income from our farm produce and a happy family life, but during the partition of India, my grandparents and parents moved to the East Panjab region of India. The partition was a sad and scary time in history for all Panjabi Indian and Muslim families who experienced a vast amount of blood, hatred, murder whilst crossing the lands. The preparation to travel had to be instant, the longer you hesitated, the higher the tensions around the village grew, the longer you waited, the higher the risk that the family would not survive. My family had such a short amount of time to cross the border under a chaotic and inhumane circumstances. They gathered their precious possessions and went on a 5-day journey to the Indian side of the border.

Our family was a Jatt family, which meant that our ancestors were traditional farmers. The caste system in India was based on your occupation, i.e., born into Farmers, carpenters, clothing, singers/musicians, goldsmiths, etc.

My mother told me that our Muslim neighbours helped the Sikh and Hindu families cross the border during the night. They had grown up together and were close friends; it broke their hearts when the partition was declared by the British/ Indian Government. She explained how her friends were kidnapped, girls disappeared... All you could hear was crying all around the village. She explained how difficult it was for our Muslim friends to help us escape the village – gangs were trying to burn down houses, hurt and split families and take over the land that wasn't theirs. It was also happening on the Indian side. However, she explained how they somehow managed to escape and lived without food and water for days, only carrying a few clothes across the border.

My parents lost all their possessions, house, farm and land. They first moved to Lohghar where my grandparents' extended family lived but had to move to the village Khanpur. The Indian government gave them an 'equivalent' plot of land in India in a village called Khanpur. It was disappointing, as there was no house, the farmland was going to take years until something grew in it, they felt deceived but had no-one to complain to. My eldest brother, Gurdeep Singh, was very young at the time he was under 12 years old. I was born a couple years after in the pre-Muslim village of Khanpur. Our family became very poor; we lived in a mud house and had no cattle, no animals and no food. My father took out a loan to feed the family and had to continue rebuilding our home after his parents passed away.

My father struggled to survive and make a living in India. He did farming but struggled on his own and needed a lot of help from family members. We survived as a family and we started school. We slowly managed our daily hardship like every other family around us.

We were really interested in our history and wanted to understand how India became as it was, what did our history say about how our ancestors lived. How did the British takeover and what life was like before them? When did the Moguls takeover India and what was lifelike with them? With so many kings and queens and empires in India, it was inspiring to see what was achieved and accomplished by the Indians.

My elder brother used to bring us storybooks about our Sikh and Hindu history from Apra (our main town Centre). He said it was important we understood our history. We read all the books about the below topics to understand the mysteries, history, poems, legends and the Gods of the past. I was interested in knowing about the Hindu Gods and their stories too. I also loved to read Panjabi and Muslim poems.

- Mirza Sahibah
- Sassi Punny
- Sohni Mahiwal
- Heer Ranjha
- Puran Bhagat, Roop Basant, Heer Warisishah, Guru Nanak's history and all the saints Hindu Gods history and stories
- Ramayan
- Mahabharat
- Zafar Nama
- Saka Sarkhand
- Saka Chamkore
- Dhadyan di mang
- Sohan Singh Seetal
- Dya Singh Dilbar

My brothers and I started singing shabad in the temple in our village, Khanpur, when there was a gathering. My elder brother, Gurdeep, played the banjo and me and Dalbir sang the hymns. We also sang in the evenings when people gathered around the fire talking about their family history.

1955 – My parents' journey to the UK

As our debt grew, my father, Sansar Singh, wanted to see if he could get into the UK to earn some money as a factory worker. There was a demand in the UK for labour in the coal mines, factories and steel works as Britain was rebuilding after the World war. The commonwealth countries had an opportunity to apply and help rebuild the country. My father took out a mortgage on the farm and also sold a small field to pay for a ticket to England to work in the factories. He had moved to Birmingham where there was a lot of demand for work in the foundries.

After three months, he wrote a letter to say that he had reached Birmingham safely. Our family was very happy and we thought we would finally become rich and pay off our debts... My father wrote how there is some tension against foreigners here but he minds his own business and tries to make a living the best he can. But this didn't happen.

After working very hard for a few years in difficult conditions, my father became very ill with TB and was admitted to hospital. My father had not sent any money and we struggled to pay off the loan and became very poor. My mother could not pay for our school fees anymore and we were sent home from school. Soon after, we started to work on the farms to help our mother, Chanan Kaur.

My Mama (mother's brother) also moved to England in 1956 and applied for a visa for my mother, to help my father. There was happiness and also sadness with us all in India. We didn't want our mother to go and cried so much. My mother also cried and said it would help us all and make our lives better if she went. She promised to get us over to England as soon as she could.

My mother got to England in 1963 and found where my father was. My father was in and out of hospital and worked when he could. She nursed him better and he became well enough to work full time again. My mother decided to work and started to sew garments for wholesalers and also worked in a factory.

My young memories of India

I thought about my mum every day. My mother used to sing at Lady Sangeet family parties and knew a lot of Boliyan; she also loved to entertain and had a good voice. I missed her when she went to the UK. I felt lonely and missed her hugs and her roti. My elder brother made huge rotis; we all used to cry when we ate together, missing our mum.

I remember when I was very young, I had a lump on the side of my right eye that was quite big. My mother took me to 'Noor Mahal', a nearby town to my big mama's (uncle's) house and then to the hospital. The doctor did an operation near my right eye to get rid of the lump and I still remember it being extremely painful. Everybody used to ask me if I wanted to go to my Mama's house and I always said, 'No, because he's going to give me an injection.' I still have the scar on my right eye.

My Nani (nan) who lived in Noor Mahal – a city in Punjab – loved me a lot. I remember her as being really kind and always giving me money to buy Indian sweets (Besan was my favourite). I loved my Nani, she was a great woman. I had two mamas who also lived in Noor Mahal. We used to have a lot of fun with my mama's children and I remember them having good singing voices. We still love each other and are so happy whenever we meet. They also looked after us when my mum was in the UK.

I sometimes think how naughty we became while my mother was in the UK. I remember making empty pretend paper cigarettes and smoking them. My elder brother caught me smoking a fake cigarette – I got some good slaps. I never smoked, nor pretended to, after that day.

I regularly took our cattle and buffaloes to the field for the whole day and just remember singing songs and coming back home in the evenings. I only had one pair of pants, shorts and a t-shirt in which I would stay in for the whole day, enjoying the sunshine. If the cattle ever went into somebody else's field, my brother would beat us up.

I also remember swimming in a six-foot deep canal once in which we nearly drowned. My eldest brother came to check on us and beat us up for jumping into the canal, so we never did that again. Thinking about it now, it was quite funny but my elder brother must have been so worried about us without our parents, it must have been so stressful for him. I do say sorry to him now whenever I go to India to visit him. We talk about old times and how he looked after us. I probably didn't appreciate it at that time but he was a hard-working, strong and loving person.

We are three brothers and my eldest brother, Gurdeep Singh, looked after us whilst we were in India. My other brother, Dalbir, passed away in 2008, he was the second eldest.

Our brother, Gurdeep, was also a talented singer and loved music but he didn't have time to practice as we did. He used to sing with a banjo and had a really good voice. He also used to buy us singing books from the nearby town, Apra. We were interested in these stories as it helped us to create songs based on the history to sing in village gatherings. Gurdeep gave us a lot of support when we started singing in India and he also wrote songs for us with deep meaning. He sadly passed away in 2021 after falling ill.

My parents: Sansar Singh and Chanan Kaur

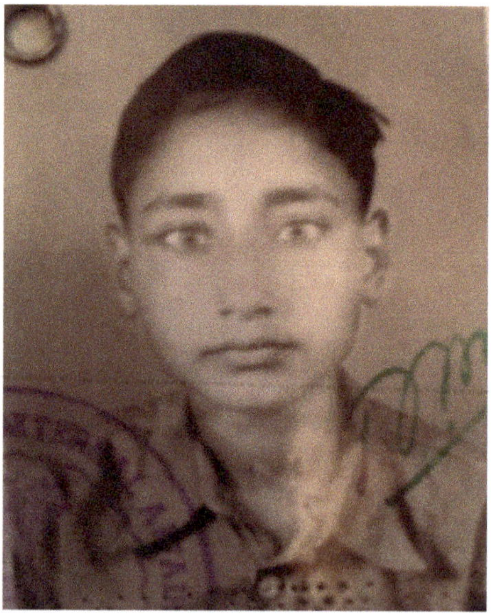

My young self

1964 – Balbir and Dalbir fly to the UK

After a difficult and painful year for all of us, my mother finally sent a letter to India and told us that me and my brother, Dalbir, could come to England and stay with her. My elder brother, Gurdeep, had to stay back to keep an eye on the house and land in the village, he was only a teenager himself.

We were so excited but also cried that we were being split up. My brother, Gurdeep, said it would be the best thing for our family and not to worry about him as he would take care of the house in India on his own. He worked really hard, he cooked and cleaned and was both a mother and father to us. He had looked after us since my father had gone to the UK.

We started to pack our things and got ready to go to England. I packed my tumbi, which I still have today, and my songbooks and storybooks. My brother packed our clothes. Both of us went to the city to get our paperwork, our injections and to confirm our single tickets.

We travelled by train, which took approximately five hours from Panjab to Delhi. My brother, Gurdeep, and my uncle, and the travel agent were with us. Once we got to Delhi, we realised we had forgotten the injection certificate book at home. My brother went back to Panjab to get the injection book. We stayed in the travel agent's house in Delhi. The flight was the next day anyway, luckily. However, someone told us that we could have just got a certificate book from a surgery in Delhi but we didn't know and there was a panic to get it in time. It must have been so frustrating and stressful for my brother to sort this out for us. We waited and waited and fell asleep hoping he gets back in time. It was a massive relief that he got to Delhi in the early hours.

I came to the UK in early 1964. It was very cold but looked so clean compared to our home village. There was no central heating in those days. Every house had a chimney and a fireplace in most rooms, even in the bedrooms. The house we lived in was rented and very small but it was enough for us.

My father used to put a fire on every day, with coal and wood, mainly in our front sitting room where the whole family would sit around it. My mother would hang washed clothes around the fire to dry. After 9pm, we would all go to bed and used hot water bottles to keep warm. It was strange and alien but we were all together as a family, which was perfect for us. We missed our brother in India very much. My mum would call the neighbours to help write a letter to India so we could let our brother know how we were. It would sometimes take 2-3 weeks for the letter to reach India.

My brother, Dalbir, went to work straight away in the foundry with my cousin on Dartmouth Road in Smethwick, Birmingham. Before we left the house, he would help clean the fireplace and start the fire before he left for work.

A week after my arrival, my mother walked me to the school. I started in Sandwell School near the Albion football ground. There were only two Asian lads in the entire school and it was full of white English people. They really hated us and we were bullied by them within two weeks of starting. They all thought we were Black and called us Nigerians. They didn't know who we were or anything about Sikhs, Hindus or Muslims. In their eyes, we were Black people and were not allowed to go and play in certain playgrounds and walk on certain streets.

Every day, the bullies would call us names and would tell us to go back to our own country. They beat us up in the playground most days. I would turn up to school late on purpose to prevent getting punched in the back or kicked.

Within a few months, a lot of other Asians also came to the school and we started to form our own little gang. We caught whoever hit us in the playground after school and beat them back. However, there were still a lot of white lads so we were still scared. Six of us Asians were in the lowest set and were being taught the alphabet and basic English, to be honest we picked it up quite quickly from all the bullying. The teacher got the cane out from time to time to get us to spell correctly. It was really upsetting and rewarding at the same time, the situation just made us stronger.

As a group of lads, we found a local Indian Karate club and started to learn how to defend and block, enough to get us by and escape most of the time.

Gradually, we learnt how to fight and defend ourselves as much as we could. Most teachers were racist towards us and would call us names too. We had the cane most days and were targeted more for being disruptive. We worked hard as a group to make our parents proud and try and get a 'good' job to support our families.

Once a white lad punched me in the face and I hit him back. I was wearing a ring at the same time and I cracked his tooth before I ran off. From then on, the headmaster had forbidden any student from wearing steel rings or any jewellery.

During this time, there were many 'white' gangs around the local area in Smethwick who really hated Asians. I can remember that one gang was called "Tidy Boys", and another was called "Skinhead Nazi". We never faced any of these gangs but they were known to have dressed in bovver boots, metal belts and leather gloves. It was a scary time and we felt alone here as young teenagers. My mother would say, 'Keep away from these people and study hard so you can get good jobs when you grow up.'

We did face a lot of problems whilst living in Smethwick near the football ground, there was a fight nearly every night in the streets. When the football was on, the Albion fans would break windows and make a lot of noise. Eventually, we moved to a house near Victoria Park to get away from the area.

English people also started to gradually change and saw how hard we worked in every industry but it took some time to really integrate. They started to mix with the Asian people and work together. Our English neighbours liked the samosas and dhal my mum made so we would give them some with some roti. It helped to make friends with them.

There was a Sikh temple built in Smethwick in the early 60s but my father said that they used to pray in local halls before the temple was built. We started to attend the local gurdwara in 1964 where we attended Panjabi school and learnt music. Our teacher was Darshan Singh Bhogal, who witnessed my singing in 1964. He passed away recently. He inspired me to sing in front of the sangat – an audience in the gurdwara – and taught me how to pronounce the words. He was a great man.

Darshan Singh Bhogal

1964 – Balbir and Dalbir Smethwick Gurdwara

Me and my brother, Dalbir, started Panjabi school on the weekends within a few weeks of us being in England. It reminded us of India and the gurdwara we attended in our village back home. We felt at home when we used to come to Panjabi school. Our teacher's name was Darshan Singh Bhogal. I had been in touch with him throughout my life as he was my mentor, but recently I met my master whilst shopping after a couple of years of not seeing him which was a great coincidence. He was so happy to see me and wrote me a reference to acknowledge the time I spent with him learning and singing in the temple, in 1964. He also provided evidence of my early career. It was so sad to hear that he'd passed away.

During our time in the gurdwara, we didn't just learn how to read and write in Panjabi but also learned to play instruments and were part of the youth's kirtan (singing) group. Here I learnt the Sikh history, learnt the tabla and the harmonium, and also met a lot of my friends on a daily basis. I started to sing shabad with my brother. Me and Dalbir formed a small kirtan group and sang religious songs. It was only the two of us at the time. Every week we went to Guru Nanak Sikh Temple in Smethwick and learnt more shabads and kirtan, performing in front of the sangat (worshipers) in the main hall.

In 1966-67, Darshan Singh Bhogal lead our class and rehearsed us to perform in small kirtan groups at major religious events and during Sunday services, this is where Bhujhangy Jhata was formed, a name given by the public meaning 'Children group. We became quite famous in Smethwick gurdwara and the sangat would come and see us each week when we performed. I had such a sweet voice and my friends were very talented musicians, which made a perfect group, attracting a lot of attention. I was the lead singer of the kirtan group but everyone got a chance to sing also.

We started to be invited to sing at other gurdwaras around the UK. We became quite a famous group of young adults.

1967 – Official Bhujhangy Jhata

Over the coming years, I continued to sing kirtan with my brother and also as part of a small group of friends. We sang all over the UK in gurdwaras and small functions and pubs. We were known as Bhujhangy Group outside of the gurdwara and Bhujhangy Jhata within the gurdwara.

The gurdwara had Indian instruments but we didn't own any ourselves. You couldn't buy Indian instruments in any shops in the UK, you had to get them from India, so we bought English instruments. We brought a guitar and a drum. We mixed both the tumbi and dholki together to make something new, which was called Punjabi pop music, also known as UK Bhangra music today. Our friends from the jatha joined our group and we became a bigger Bhujhangy Group, with me as the lead singer and the others as backing singers and musicians; the other members could also sing.

We started to write songs together, mainly about our experiences in the UK and missing our home in India. We also wrote a lot of religious songs. Our main focus was folk music, explaining the environment, our feelings, traditions and way of life around us through our songs. It was exciting and scary at the same time, we had so much ambition and drive to do more and more gigs and perform wherever we could, most of the time for free. We decided to record some of our songs on a formal record and decided to travel to Uxbridge. The recordings were short and we had to record in one take. We managed to make 100 copies of our first record.

This was a 4-track recording mini record and we recorded four songs. The producers of the songs were Sukhi and Gurnam.

We came back home and labelled the record ourselves and then distributed the 100 copies around the West Midlands in Jukeboxes in pubs and clubs. This was our first recording and our first official album, distributed to a wider audience. All our publicity was through weddings and functions and word of mouth. Our music travelled all over the UK and we were known as one of the first popular bands in the UK. The public knew we had been singing in temples since 1964.

I used the name Balbir Singh *Khanpur*, as Khanpur was our village name. I wanted to make our village famous and my brother proud of our success.

In 1967, I began to work in a foundry called Walsall Conduits LTD. My job was to fetch sand in wheelbarrows, which was very difficult. Wet sand would often be extremely heavy to push and my back would also ache. I was quite skinny and not very strong at the time. We then wrote a song about pushing the barrow. It was called "Methon Bara Dhakya Na Jaye".

Factory photo

Everyone would call me to sing songs to them in the foundry to keep the mood happy and pass the time. I'd eat breakfast and then sometimes start singing for the whole of break time and then sing during lunchtime.

During this time, we were able to buy a house with partnership with my cousin sister. We paid half the money and they paid half and shared the house as 2 families. After 5 years, we had an argument and decided to move out. My father asked for the money so we could move out and buy another house, my cousin refused and said we had no evidence and the house was not on our names. We had no money to fight a case, my cousin ordered us to get out of her house. We soon moved out the house and bought another one with a loan. The house was on Oxford Street in Smethwick.

1969 – My First TV appearance

Celebrating 500th Birthday of Guru Nanak

A programme for Guru Nanak Dev Ji's 500th birthday was being planned in the Guru Nanak Sikh Temple. We were getting ready to celebrate and our teacher made a group of children sing shabads and religious songs on Guru Nanak Dev Ji's 500th birthday.

We were invited to perform on ITV in 1969 on Guru Nanak's 500th Birthday and the programme was called something along the lines of *Friends and Neighbours*, which was on ITV, in black and white at that time. From there, our group became quite popular and we were recognised a lot within our community.

Singing in temples had always been the forefront of

our career. We started at our local Sikh temple and had been performing there for about 15 years. However, because of new communities, new conditions, new rules about who can perform in a gurdwara, they didn't allow us to continue to perform in our Smethwick Sikh temple due to us not having a turban, but other gurdwaras still allowed us to perform. Of course, we performed free of charge and people would swarm the temple and even listen to us while standing outside the temple with a speakerphone broadcasting my voice.

Our group met many audiences, even the spiritual and religious ones, and when other Sikh temples found out we had stopped performing in our local temple, we were invited to other Sikh temples, including in Kent and Glasgow. Guru Ravidass is still the temple we have been performing at for the last 40+ years. I have also released an LP, a religious CD of songs specifically for Guru Ravidass. I still perform in many Guru Ravidass temples around the country, and also in Europe as people from the community love what I do and I really appreciate the support that they give me.

In 2019, I celebrated the 550th Guru Nanak Gurpurb and released a song to celebrate.

1970 – The Performer

We started recording in 1967-68 but properly released our songs with Star Agency, which is now called Oriental Star Agencies. The company released approximately all 300 of our songs and we started singing in most Sikh temples around the UK.

Some of songs did really well and others not so well, but every EP or LP was different to each other. We were trying new ideas every time. We also had some great hit albums, which are still played today. Our religious songs were more popular than our folk songs. I was really happy that people liked my voice, the songs of the group and our performances.

We performed in temples from Glasgow to Dundee, to Gravesend in London. The instruments we used were electron organ, accordion, banjo, tumbi and dholaki. In the 60s, many people came from Punjab, India and most of the men went to the pub to spend time after a hard day's work in the foundry. We started to entertain them in the pub in 1967 by singing without a microphone. However, our father wasn't too happy about us singing as a profession. He wanted us to study not sing and waste time. We had long arguments about singing in pubs, but we didn't stop singing. We stood on tables and benches in the pub and started to sing songs about life in England with my tumbi. I remember singing the songs "Puban wich jana shaddeh" (Stop going to the pub) and "Tor walaytan di" (The walk of a British lady).

1971–1973 – I bought my first car

I began working near Birmingham town centre in 1971. We had to buy bicycles in order to get there and faced many difficult situations. I remember falling off my bike once in the middle of the road and nearly getting run over. I then decided that I needed to learn how to drive and would take lessons, costing 50p each at that time. After failing a few times, I finally passed my driving test in 1972. My brother and I worked together in a factory and we bought a car to make transport a lot easier for us. I eventually taught him how to drive and he went on to passing his driving test as well.

In my early days, I was a proper Sikh; I had long hair, wore a turban, never shaved and would go to the temple every week. However, I had to cut my hair to find work otherwise no one was hiring me, it was necessary at the time.

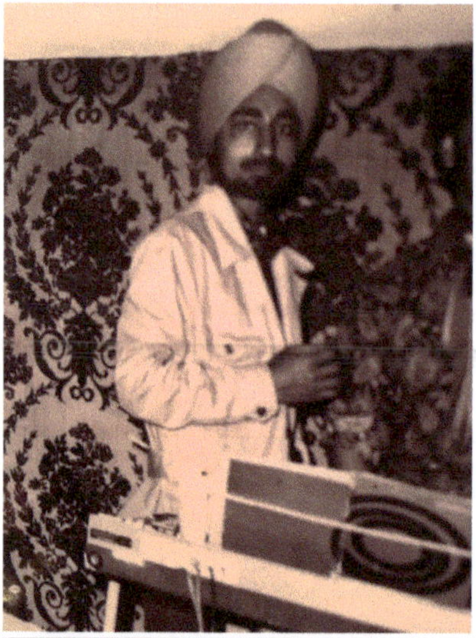

Dhian Dhan Wegana
ਧੀਆਂ ਧਨ ਵਿਗਾਨਾ
Viah De Geet
ਵਿਆਹ ਦੇ ਗੀਤ
Marriage Songs
Balbir Singh Khanpur
Dalbir Singh Khanpur
Rajinder Singh Dhanohi

Tor Walaytan Di
Balbir Singh Khanpur

1975 – Asian Song Contests Start

In 1975, Oriental Star Agencies organised the first Asian Song Contest in the UK. It was held in Coventry and so many groups and individuals took part in the event. It was so nice to see the variety of music groups. After that year, I took part in every song contest and won many trophies and medals.

Bhujhangy Group of Smethwick.
Balbir Singh of Bhujhangy Group,
Asian song contest 1975

ORIENTAL STAR AGENCIES
BIRMINGHAM

presents

ASIAN SONG CONTEST
(U.K.) 1975

at

DIGBETH CIVIC HALL
DERITEND, BIRMINGHAM

on

Saturday, 17th May 1975 at 6-00 p.m.

ADMISSION FEE
50p.

№ 0614

The trip to Glasgow

The Indian Workers Association had branches around the UK and abroad. They celebrated and organised shows on a yearly basis. I can remember one show that they organised in Glasgow and the whole show was free. We have been to Glasgow many times and knew it like the back of our hands. We had fans all over the country who would come this event especially to see us perform.

As usual, a van was hired for the long-distance drive and we headed to Glasgow for a charity show. We filled up on petrol halfway to the event and realised the van was diesel. The van stopped on the motorway and we realised what we had done. Not wanting to let our fans down, we emptied the van ourselves and walked back to the service station to get the right diesel. But, by the time we drove to Glasgow, the show was over and people had left. We got there and the organiser was still happy to see us, even though we missed his event. It was a funny memory despite us feeling shameful and it was entirely the drivers fault for putting in petrol instead of diesel.

1977 – I got Married

In 1977, I had an arranged marriage with Amarjit Kaur, who I call Ambi. My mother went to India to look for a wife for me, and after a few weeks, she came back to England and said, 'I have arranged your marriage.'

I don't think I had a reaction at the time. I thought it was a good idea and looked forward to having a wife. I wrote her many love poems and would secretly post them to India; it was a funny experience.

I sponsored her and filled in the paperwork, and after a few months, I went to the airport and saw her for the first time. At the airport, she said to me, 'I was told to look for a short man with big heels.' I didn't think I was that short but we laughed and were quite shy with each other.

My father

Our wedding was arranged during the couple of weeks after her arrival, so she helped me fix up the house and paint it before we had our temple wedding. We had many guests staying at our house for the two weeks. It was a simple wedding in Smethwick Gurdwara and my brother and friends sang in the temple. We had no venue, so the men went to the pub after the temple and the women sang and danced at home.

We've been together for over 45 years now, with four children and six grandchildren. Amarjit cares a lot for me and we both understand each other.

In the same year, I remember us taking part in an Asian song contest, which was held at Wembley Conference Centre in London. I rehearsed every day as the contests were quite tough. If you sang an original, you got a lot of points. If you sang gazals you got even more points, however, if you sang gazals in light classical raags, you got even more points. Extra points were also given if you sang in Urdu and wore Asian clothes.

We went to an Urdu writer Jagmohan Joshi who was the general secretary of IWA – the Indian Worker Association. He wrote many classical Ghazals for me and taught me how to pronounce certain words which took a lot of practice.

There was a classical singer called Gurdial Singh Rasia, who knew many raags. He fixed the Urdu Ghazal into a raag called 'Yaman Kalyan' and taught me how to sing in certain raags and themes. I also had the best tabla player, Arshid Malik, from Pakistan.

Every day I practiced, recited and improved my vocabulary and pronunciation until the day before the competition. All the group members stayed over at my house and slept in the living room, we were all excited and focused at the same time, we wanted to win.

The next morning, we went to London for the competition. I sang and performed very well. We did lose a point on our dress, we did not wear the traditional salvar kameez, like Pathan wear, but wore our Bhujhangy group uniform. We came second, losing by only one point. This contest was shown on TV and everybody had said that we performed very well. I will never forget the day of that competition. It motivated me to take part in the following competitions that were organised. There are some YouTube videos released by Media Take and Oriental Star Agencies. We continued to come First or in the Top 3 for many years, something we looked forward to participating in.

STAR RECORDS
Birmingham UK
Tel. 021-440-2445
SIDE 2
M.C.P.S.
℗1977
Made In U.K.
(Zel.EPS.204-B)
JHEPS.204
SR.116
45 r p m Stereo
BHUJHANGY GROUP
"Mere Ishq Kahani Ki Poochdan Ay"
(Lyrics: Bhujhangy)
singer: Balbir Singh
music direction: Bhujhangy Group
Recorded and Produced by
Zella Recording Studios
Birmingham, England

STAR RECORDS
Birmingham UK
Tel. 021-440-2445
SIDE 1
M.C.P.S.
℗1977
Made In U.K.
(Zel.EPS.204-A)
JHEPS.204
SR.116
45 r p m Stereo
BHUJHANGY GROUP
1. "Walayati Main Taan Peeni Aa" (Lyrics: Bhujangy Gp.)
2. "Bhabhi Munda Lambran Da (Lyrics: P. L. Jhally)
singer: Balbir Singh
music direction: Bhujhangy Group
Recorded and Produced by
Zella Recording Studios
Birmingham, England

1979 – My Mother dies, my trip to India

Me, my wife, and our two children, along with my brother, Dalbir, his wife and two children, lived in the same house with my mum and dad. We lived in a two-bedroom terraced house with a bedroom in the attic. We had no baths in our house and used to go to the local swimming centre once a week to have a wash. It was the normal way of life. We did have the money to buy a bigger house but it never occurred to us to separate or look for a house. We continued as we were, working twelve hours a day, seven days a week, to provide for our growing family.

My mother had suffered from cancer but no one in the family knew about it except her. Sadly, she died from cancer in 1979 and she wished for her body to be taken to India. It took us ten weeks to organise. It was a very painful time to arrange this as we were still performing and couldn't let people down at the last minute. She said she didn't like funeral boxes and wanted her funeral to be done in her village in open air. A few weeks after asking her about her will, she passed away. Despite the pain and sorrow at that time, me and my brother, Dalbir Singh, discussed it and decided that I should take her body to India.

When I reached the Delhi Airport, the officers weren't ready to release my mother's body. They sent me around many places, to many people, and I remember sitting in the airport for hours. My big brother, Gurdeep Singh, then told me that they wanted money to release the body. I told them to their faces directly that I wasn't willing to pay a single penny and after hours they finally released her body, which we took in a box from Delhi to Punjab. My mother had told us to never leave our jobs and to always work hard and be honest. She was a divine woman who always had a smile on her face and would always sacrifice anything for her family.

We were glad that we managed to fulfil my mother's last wish. When I reached the Delhi Airport with my mother's body, my older brother, Gurdeep Singh, came to collect me and my mother. We hired a taxi from Delhi to Punjab and travelled all night. In the morning, we were at our village, Khanpur. As she had wished, the funeral was done at her village in open air. From that day, I became a vegetarian and stopped drinking.

At the same time, the rest of the Bhujhangy team were also travelling to India, but to Bombay. We were asked to perform at a Vaisakhi event. After the funeral, I travelled to Bombay to meet the rest of the team.

In Bombay, we stayed in the house of a famous Bollywood actor, named Pran. He was such a generous and kind man, he was nothing like his evil character in Hindi films. It was such a great experience; we spent a lot of money, had a great time, had lots of fun and really enjoyed it. Pran had introduced us to Laxmikant Payerelal, a music director of Hindi films. Laxmikant asked to hear our voice and if he liked it, he would give us a chance to sing in a movie. My mother would have been so proud of us for reaching Bombay and living our dream. He asked me to stay behind for another few weeks but I couldn't leave my family.

We were treated like stars and lived in Pran's house, where we were given access to his swimming pool (all new to us) and free drinks, food and a chance to perform in front of thousands of people.

One song I remember singing was a religious LP and the other was Punjabi folk. They really liked us so they gave us the opportunity to sing in the movie and I was so honoured but he wanted us to stay and live in Bombay. I had to refuse and say no thank you as my family and children were in the UK. After our trip to Bombay, our whole group caught a flight to Delhi. We arrived back at London Heathrow airport, knowing we would never get the chance to go back to India again to sing. This may have been the biggest mistake I had made but, at the time, it was the right decision to come back to my family.

We were the lead singers and we kept on going and performing across the UK. We had many musicians come and go in the group and some successfully created their own bands. I sang over 300 songs, including religious songs, ghazals and traditional folk songs.

1980s – Life Goes on....

There was a new chapter in my life without my mother, my rock. I missed her so much, my dad wasn't very well either.

A special memory in 1980 was when we went to see my Bhua Ji and Phupar Ji in Coventry (my wife's uncle and aunty). We got there and our Bhua Ji told us that Baba Ji was coming to see the sangat so I should wait for an hour. I waited and when I asked again, she told me that they were already here and were sitting in the front room. I had expected Baba Ji to be dressed in orange-coloured clothes but when I saw them I was surprised because they were sitting in a three-piece suit with a tie on. He was very friendly and his name was Baba Ajit Singh. We laughed, joked around, and I really respected him a lot. I went to sing in the Ajit Darbar temple many times as well. He has passed away now but I really remember him and the time that I had spent with him. Now he is no more but he is with us all the time.

ਮੁਕਾਬਲੇ ਵਿਚ ਪਹਿਲਾ ਨੰਬਰ ਲੈ ਕੇ ਇਕ ਵਾਰ ਫਿ
ਖਾਨਪੁਰ ਨੇ ਮਿਡਲੈਂਡਜ਼ 'ਚ ਧੁੰਮਾਂ ਪਾ ਦਿੱਤ
ਬਲਬੀਰ ਖਾਨਪੁਰ ਗਰੁੱਪ ਦਾ ਰੀਕਾਰਡ
ਧੀਆਂ ਧਨ ਬਿਗਾਨਾ
ਸਾਰੇ ਇੰਗਲੈਂਡ 'ਚ ਸਫਲਤਾ ਦੇ ਝੰਡੇ ਗੱਡ ਰਿਹਾ ਹੈ
ਜੇਕਰ ਤੁਸੀ ਅਜੇ ਤਕ ਨਹੀਂ ਖ਼ਰੀਦਿਆ ਤਾਂ ਅੱਜ ਹੀ ਖ਼ਰੀਦੋ

021-
1408

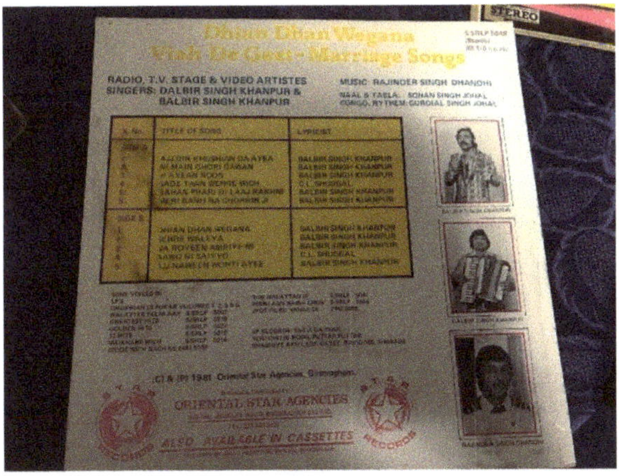

Many cassettes and albums released over the years

1982 – Trip to Europe

A friend of ours booked a show for us in Paris. The whole group travelled in advance on the ferry, however, when we reached the French border, we were all stopped by Immigration. They were stopping us from passing through the French border because all our passports were Indian, not British. The whole group had Indian passports and we had asked the organisers of the show whether we needed to apply for a visa, but they said we didn't. Immigration kept us for 48 hours in separate rooms until matters were sorted. We were sent back on the ferry without doing our show and everyone was very disappointed. After that we all decided to apply for a British passport so these kinds of issues didn't occur again. We then continued to have shows arranged in other countries without needing a British passport, including Germany, France and Canada.

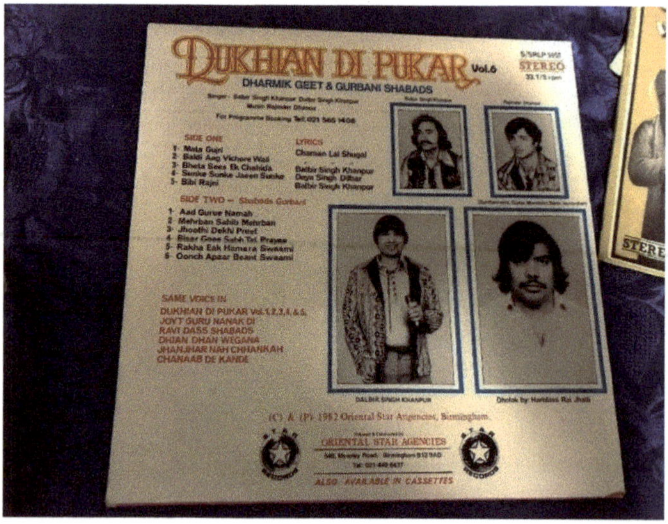

1979 – 1987 My children

I have four children: my son, Jetender (Thind), my daughter, Sutender (Satty), my younger daughter, Parvinder (Parv/ET), and my son, Sukhjinder (Rocky). My children have been around music since they were born. When my elder two children were born, I was performing on stage and rushed to the maternity ward after the performances. I was present when my younger two were born.

My younger daughter was the most interested in music and loved to play alongside me on stage when she was very young. I have always encouraged my children to pick up an instrument and play. My daughter, Parv, picked up the dhol, the drums, tabla and the piano. She was very passionate and now has her own company – Eternal Taal. She plays and teaches the dhol and also provides dance lessons and fitness classes. She has an all-female dance and drumming group and has been performing for over 25 years now.

My Grandchildren are Simran, Amrit, Aman, Harpreet, Jaspreet and Jaya. They are also musical and play the Piano, Viola & Violin. The dogs in the family are two German Shepherds. My daughter-in-law Raj is a very good TV presenter and has done many radio shows and interviews which has been great as a family.

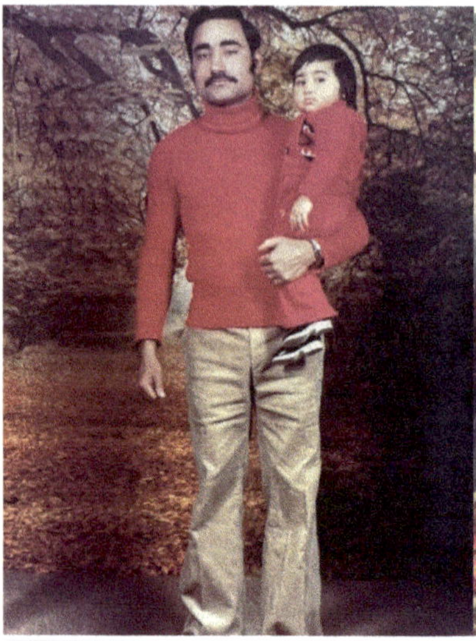

My daughter Satty and my Son Jetender

My younger son Sukhjinder (Rocky)
My elder son Jetender Singh, his wife Rajwinder Kaur, their three daughters: Simran, Amrit and Aman Fagura

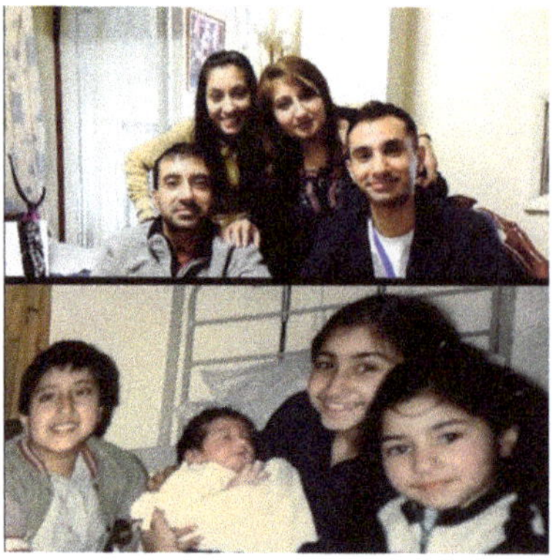

My four children

My six grand children

My younger daughter Parvinder (Parv) Kaur established her own Entertainment group of just women. She became a professional international Dhol player performing in three Bollywood movies, Glastonbury, Graham Norton show, various charity events and weddings all over the world. I am so proud of her and also my granddaughters Simran, Amrit and Aman who are also playing Dhol in Eternal Taal.

Parv Kaur (daughter)

Simran, Amrit & Aman
(Granddaughters)

EternalTaal.com established in 1999

1985 – My father, Sansar Singh

My Father died in 1985, he was in his late 70s. He hadn't really been well for a number of years, many chest infections caused by years working in the factory and also smoking didn't help. The funeral was held in Birmingham, he didn't have any last wishes for his ashes but we took his ashes to Kiratpur Gurdwara in the north of India.

1990s – Our Silver Jubilee

I remember recording a jingle for a radio show based on the Hindi film *Jhuk Gaya Aasman, "kaun hai jo sapnu mein ayea"*. We went to a radio station for an interview and sang on Diwali, Guru Nanak Dev Ji's birthday and Vaisakhi. The presenter was very friendly and we had a good time.

In this era, DJs became more popular than live bands. They were flexible and played so many songs and such a variety of music that the live bands started to fade out. Time had changed in this era. The young generation were being creative and taking over us.

We celebrated our silver jubilee, for 25 years of Bhujhangy Group. I went to Sidhu and asked if he could arrange it at the Dome in Birmingham. He ordered trophies as well and there were tickets to see the show at the Dome. Lots of people came to see the show and there were also many artists who performed. Mohammed Ayuab was also there and he presented Bhujhangy Group with a trophy to commemorate our silver jubilee. This was an unforgettable night. Thanks to all UK artists of the UK, and also OSA, who released a video of the silver jubilee.

Many singers in the industry are good at miming when they need to. We tried this once at a meal fair in Cannon Hill Park. They called us on stage, we had our tape cassettes and decided to mime. The tapes were put in , my brother Dalbir Singh and I started to move our lips and dance on stage without actually singing. The tape stopped halfway through and people found out that we weren't actually singing, we were miming. They were very upset, and we had to come off stage. It was a really embarrassing day for us and since then we decided that we would never mime again. We would sing live no matter what. People should enjoy live bands and live music so I always sing on top of the CD if I have to but cannot mime.

2008 – My brother, Dalbir, leaves me

On the morning of 28th November 2008, I got a phone call from my wife and she told me that Bhaji Dalbir Ji was no more. I asked her how she knew and she had said that somebody had phoned her. As soon as I heard this news, I came home immediately and went straight to Dudley Road hospital. I saw him, my brother, lying on the trolley bed with an open mouth. The doctor said that he had had a heart attack and they tried to save him but couldn't. I was very shocked and went to the toilets and cried for my brother. We had been together all our life we weren't just brothers, we were best friends. We had never tried to fight each other and sang together for 40 years. This was it and he had just suddenly passed away. It was a very upsetting time for me and my family.

I was so frightened on the inside but remained strong for others around me. During that day, and for days before the funeral, we had visitors coming to the house to pay their respects to the one we dearly lost. I didn't eat for a whole day as I didn't feel hungry or thirsty at this time. My wife was worried about me and I needed to have energy in me to maintain my calm amongst all these visitors.

A few months later, I went to India to disperse the ashes. My older brother, Gurdeep, came with us and he was very upset. We went to the gurdwara and did the ceremony and let him go... It was a difficult time and my brother was gone forever. Once somebody goes, they never come back... And just stay as a memory. He was my good brother and friend. Despite living in separate houses with our own families, we'd stayed together our whole lives as friends and helped each other. I miss him all the time.

2009 – Going Solo – Golden Jubilee

A magazine in London called *Eastern Eye* started to research and came to the Midlands to speak to Oriental Star Agency; they found out that Bhujhangy were the pioneers of Bhangra music in the UK. They wrote in the *Eastern Eye* magazine that this was 300 years after the birth of Khalsa. We were also phoned by Guinness World Records and asked details of when we recorded our first song in the UK. My name was put on page one of the 2001 Guinness book. In 2011, I was the longest playing bhangra band in the UK. I went to India and recorded a cassette called *Tumba and Dhol,* in Jalandhar in a studio called the Rippy studio.

2012

Ram Sroop phoned us to ask us to come and sing at the Ravidass temple in Walsall. We, as a group, went to Walsall, to the Guru Ravidass temple, with all our instruments and asked for Ram Sroop. They told us that he had gone to India and we said that we were asked to come and sing here. The secretary of the stage told us that we weren't booked and they didn't need our group. We pleaded and asked for them to give us five minutes as it was insulting because we were being watched by various people. He agreed and we sang a song and came back home blaming each other.

On 26th February, we celebrated Guru Ravidass Ji's Birthday. I was called and asked to come and I did free sewa in the Hindu mandir as the temple was closed because of building purposes. We sang in many committees, including a Hindu temple, Ravidass temple, Darshan Dass temple, Satsang Baba Balak Nath temple and Nirankari temple. We also sang at a Christian church, for a congress party and Akali party.

I also attended the Punjabian Di Balle Balle programme. Me, Mall and Anary went to their studios, sang songs and were interviewed about G.Mall's new single called "Saarey Dillo". Before this single, G.Mall phoned me to say that he was releasing a new single and wanted me to record on it as well. I said no problem and went to see Mall in his house and hear the new single, as well as record my own part. He was very pleased and we arranged the interview following this. This programme was also shown on TV. G.Mall was very helpful to us in the programme and I'd known him for over 30 years. He is a good, friendly person who's always smiling and respects us a lot.

In October, we performed on Sangat TV. My teacher from 1964, Darshan Singh Bhogal, rang me and said he wanted to interview me and wanted me to sing a few songs. We went to Sangat TV and started the interview as I usually would; I spoke about my journey of coming to the UK in 1964 and singing in Smethwick Sikh temple. I also mentioned him teaching us Punjabi, shabads, religious songs, and when we performed on TV on Guru Nanak Dev Ji's 500th Birthday in 1969. After the interview, I sang three songs with my tumbi. That night was very memorable as I performed on TV with my teacher after 43 years. Many people phoned me to congratulate me on my performance and they said that they hadn't heard my voice since 1964 and this was quite sweet of them. After this, I touched my teacher's feet and he gave me blessings. I really respect my teacher as he gave me a big opportunity in 1969. He made me who I was and inspired me to sing as the Bhujhangy Jhata.

I was invited to perform on a show in the town hall. We went to the town hall and there were video cameras and people asking us whether we had come to watch the show. We told them that we were the pioneers of bhangra music and our name was also featured in the Guinness Book of World Records in 2001. My daughter (leader of ETERNAL TAAL) also performed with me in a few shows and we made a good team. She played the Dhol and I sang. People were very happy and loved our performance. Pritam was playing the tabla and he was known as the best tabla player in the whole of the West Midlands. I remember that he used to play dholak but unfortunately his hand was cut when playing this and started to bleed. He then gave it up and started on the tabla. He was only a kid then and now he's a master at the tabla. Generally, the show was amazing and I really enjoyed it.

On 6th October, I rang Brit Asia to nominate Bhujhangy for an award for being the longest running group in the UK. We went to the awards show and as soon as we walked in there was media everywhere – reporters, paparazzi and interviewers. We stood for photos, facing camera flashes that came from all around. There was lots of applause and we told them that we were the pioneers of Punjabi music and our name was featured in the Guinness Book of World Records. We sang two or three songs in front of the camera and then at 7pm went into the main hall. Free bags of basmati rice were placed under all the chairs. I took three bags as a lot of food was wasted that day. There were about 50 artists and singers but they didn't get any awards. This may have been because we were already awarded the achievement of being the longest playing band in 2011. Prithvi Singh Azad MP, Government of India, gave us an award for our singing success and for the first ever recording of the Guru Ravidass shabad in1970.

Throughout my life I learnt to play a range of instruments. The first instrument I ever played was the tumbi and I still have my 45-year-old string tumbi that I'd brought from India in my attic. I then progressed to the harmonium, which I gradually picked up. I then moved on to learning how to play the banjo with my left hand. I managed learning how to play bits of the Hawaiian guitar, Spanish guitar, and bass guitar. Alongside this, I would play dholaki, a little bit of tabla, and dhol. I've also attempted the sarangi, sitar and dhad accordion. These were all very hard instruments to play. Your own voice is also an instrument and can be very difficult to maintain.

We had people from loads of different communities and cultures play several instruments for our group, including English guitar, Jamaican bass, a Muslim tabla player, a Hindu dholak player, a Sikh dhol Player, and female vocalists.

Famous people I have met and seen:

Mohammed Rafi
Dara Singh
Lata Mangeshkar
Jamla Jatt
Hazar Singh Ramta
Surinder Kaur
Prakash Kaur
Asa Singh Mastana
Kuldip Manak
Gurdass Maan
Pran (actor)
Bhappi Lahiri
Laxmikant Pyarelal
Sunny Deol
Dharmendra
Ustaad Nusrat Fateh Ali Khan
Alam Lohar
Gulam Ali
Satinder Sartaj
Jane McDonald
And many more....

Taals I can sing in:

Dadra (6 beat)
Kehrwa (8 beat)
Rupak (7 beat)
Deep Chand Chenchal (7 or 14)
Jhap (10 beat)
Teen Taal (16 beat)
9 beat

Raags I can sing in:

Yaman Kalyaan
Darbari Kanra
Bhairu
Bharivi
Talang
Pahari
Bhopali
Shiv Ranjni
Todi
10 Thaths for raags
Arohi and Avvrohi for raags
Badi and Sambadi

I'd like to thank all radios stations and TV stations that have supported me for over 55 years.

Awards – latest to earliest

2022: Featured in the documentary 'Back In Time for Birmingham' by Noreen Khan BB2

2022: British Sikh Awards 2022

2021: Guinness Book of World Records, performing as Bhujhangy continuously since 1967

2020: UK Bhangra Awards – Best Song writer 2020

2019: Guinness Book of World Records Participant in the 550 musicians performing for the Gurpurb of Guru Nanak Dev Ji.

2019: Guinness Book of World Records for continuously performing every year for 50 years as an artist - Balbir Bhujhangy.

2019: Baba Balak Nath Ji Mandir – Performance for celebrating 15th Anniversary

2019: Nominated for Birmingham Music Awards

2018: BBC did a documentary in 2018 called *Pump up the Bhangra*, featuring Balbir Singh. Video link attached: https://youtu.be/d1b-K3anInc

2018: Birmingham Music Awards – Balbir Singh was nominated.

2016: BBC also did a documentary in 2016 called *Sikhs of Smethwick* featuring Balbir Singh. https://youtu.be/9FpYJ-ZPsKQ

2015: The UK Bhangra Awards presented a 'Special Contribution Award'

2013: Awarded for continuously singing for 22 years singing at the Yamla Jatt Mela

2011: Guinness Book of World Records – Balbir Singh performing since 1967 – to date (2011)

2011: Brit Asia awarded Balbir a Lifetime Achievement award.

2009: Balbir was awarded a House of Commons award for his services in the Indian Music Industry and Community.

2007: Medal for lifetime achievement award for over 40 years in the industry from Lal Chand Yamla Jatt N.C Trust.

2001: Guinness Book of World Records 2001: (Balbir Singh – Pioneer of Bhangra Music in the UK)

2005: Guinness Book of world Records 2005: (Balbir Singh - LONGEST RUNNING BHANGRA BAND)

2009: Vaisakhi sponsored by South Birmingham College

2007: Lal Chand Yamla Jatt, Cultural Trust UK, Presented by Nirmal Razai Mart of Co LTD (Bradford)

2006-2011 (yearly award): Guest of Honour presented by Lui Chand Yamla Jatt Cultural Trust UK

2005: Guest of Honour presented by Lal Chand Yamla Jatt Cultural Trust UK 2005 Sponsored by Dhaliwal Construction LTD

2004: 1 May, Punjabi Cultural Society UK & UCC Group Present this award to honour your outstanding contributions to the Punjabi Culture and Music presented by his holiness. Sai Bhajan Ji Kadri.

2003: 'Guest of Honour' presented by Lal Chand Yamla Jatt Cultural Trust UK 2003

2002: Shri Guru Ravidass temple, Walsall

2001: Asian Language Service

2000: Presented by Lai Chand Yamla Jatt, Cultural Trust UK

1998: Contestant OF Zee Addicts, Nov/Dec 98

1998: The Council of Sikh Gurdwaras, Birmingham Vaisakhi

1997/1998: Shri Guru Ravi Das Sabha, Paris (France) Guest of Honour Shri Guru Ravidass Bhawan 97-Rue Anatole 93120 LA-Gourneuve, France Tel: 4838 2188

1996: Shri Guru Ravidass Bhawan, Union Row, Handsworth, Birmingham B21 9EN, England, U.K.
Tel: 0121 523 9593

1995-1996: Rai & Dosanjh Entertainment Presents Shaheed Bhagat-Singh Anniversary

1995: Presented by S.H. Guru Ravidass Sabha UK, H.O. Guru Ravidass Bhawan Union Row, Handsworth B-21 9EN

1993: Entasia Management LTD, NU-TEK AHIDO ENT & Big Baba presents 1993, for Best Producers and Folk era

1992: Bhujhangy group celebrates 25 years of Bhangra music at The Dome – 16/12/92 awards

1987: Best Male Singer, 1st place, 10th Asian Song Contest, UK. Guest Star Pammi Bakhshi, by Oriental Star Agencies

1986/87: Asian Pop Awards Outstanding contribution. 1st place, by Oriental Star Agencies, Birmingham

1983: Asian Song Contest Balbir Singh Singing performance – 'Yeh Dilbar he Mehboob Mehra'
Performance on YouTube: https://www.youtube.com/watch?v=QdfsFsVQ1sM

1982: Asian Song Contest – Finalist, by Oriental Star Agencies, Birmingham

1981: Asian Song Contest Birmingham, Digbeth Civic Hall, 3rd place, by Oriental Star Awards.

1977: Asian Song Content, Silver Jubilee – Runner up, by Oriental Star Agencies, Birmingham

1976: Asian Song Contest at the BBC Shepherd's Bush Television Centre

1969: ITV Television performance Celebrating 500th Birthday of Guru Nanak

Bhujhangy

TERE ISHQ
BALBIR BHUJHANGY ft. RAVI BAL

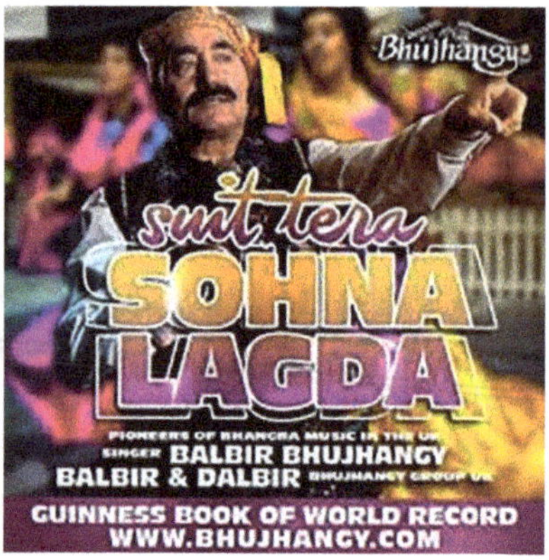
Bhujhangy
suit tera
SOHNA
LAGDA
SINGER BALBIR BHUJHANGY
BALBIR & DALBIR
GUINNESS BOOK OF WORLD RECORD
WWW.BHUJHANGY.COM

GUINNESS WORLD RECORDS

2020 – During Covid

One of my dear friends, close family member, passed away just before Covid in a tragic car accident in 2019. I was approached by the family to write a song in his memory in January 2020. Over the coming months, the lockdowns around the world started to happen and Covid became a "real" thing which shook the world. I started to write the lyrics for the song "Daddy Bina", meaning "without dad" but I couldn't go to any studio to record the lyrics. I worked with the music producer and my two daughters. We collated musicians from India and UK and recorded it all online during April and May. During June, I managed to book a studio in isolation for a few hours and record the vocals. During June, the music video was being created and the promotion material finalised. This was a truly digital experience, which was a first for me – normally I travel to India and speak to the music video producers but it was all done online and managed remotely. This was a massive team effort with the family, my daughters, the music producers and the musicians. The song was released on 1st August 2020 and was a heart-touching success. The heartache was felt in my lyrics for all families that had lost their loved ones during the pandemic.

I continued to record remotely for various events and also released a song about Covid to promote social distancing and staying indoors during the pandemic. It is a traditional way for me to write songs on what's happening at the the current time. It's a type of folk song, songs about the people, the environment the way of life today.

GUINNESS WORLD RECORDS
2019

INFINITY MUSIC
PRESENTS
ਐਸੀ ਲਾਲ ਤੁਝ ਬਿਨੁ ਕਉਨੁ ਕਰੈ
AISI LAL TUJH BIN KAUN KARE
(Shabad Shri Guru Ravidass Ji Maharaj)
SINGER
BALBIR BHUJHANGY GROUP UK
MUSIC: HARBANS AZAAD VIDEO: YRS MEDIA UK
LABEL INFINITY MUSIC

INFINITY MUSIC UK
PRESENTS
ਦੇਹ ਸ਼ਿਵਾ ਬਰ ਮੋਹਿ
DEH SHIVA BAR MOHE
SINGER
BALBIR BHUJHANGY GROUP UK
MUSIC & VIDEO: YRS MEDIA UK
LABEL INFINITY MUSIC UK

INFINITY MUSIC
PRESENTS
SATGUR NANAK PARGTEYA
ਸਤਿਗੁਰ ਨਾਨਕ ਪ੍ਰਗਟਿਆ
SINGER
BALBIR BHUJHANGY GROUP UK.
LABEL
INFINITY MUSIC
MUSIC
HARBANS AZAAD
EDITOR
AKSHAY VERMA
VIDEO
KAMAL MEHTAN

Main Nankane Jawan
550
Singer: Balbir Singh Bhujhangy Group
Lyrics: Balbirbhujhangy
Music: Arjinder Kang
Video: Bill Kooner (Bill Media Enterprises)
music minds
Released By Music Minds LTD
Tel: +44 (0) 7973 164129 Email: info@musicminds.tv

Jai Mazdoor Jai Kisan

'Jai Mazdoor Jai Kisan' has been written and sung by the legendary singer Balbir Singh Bhujhangy. This is a heartfelt plea to help our farmers in India who are struggling with justice and wellbeing.

Music by Harbans Azaad - Released by Infinity Music Ltd
Link to song: https://www.youtube.com/watch?v=eIpc5cVP6zY
Please visit: www.bhujhangy.com
Facebook: Official – Bhujhangy Group since 1967

Presented an award for the Kisan Song

2022 – Platinum Jubilee

I am proud to say my daughter Park Kaur and my granddaughter Simran Kaur Fagura got the opportunity to perform at the Platinum Jubilee celebrations in London.

I give my blessing to the next generations promoting Bhangra.

18:34
4G
Instagram
bbcnews
BBC NEWS
39,964 likes
bbcnews The Queen appeared surrounded by Prince Charles and Camilla, and Prince William and Catherine with their three children, as her Platinum Jubilee celebrations drew to a close.

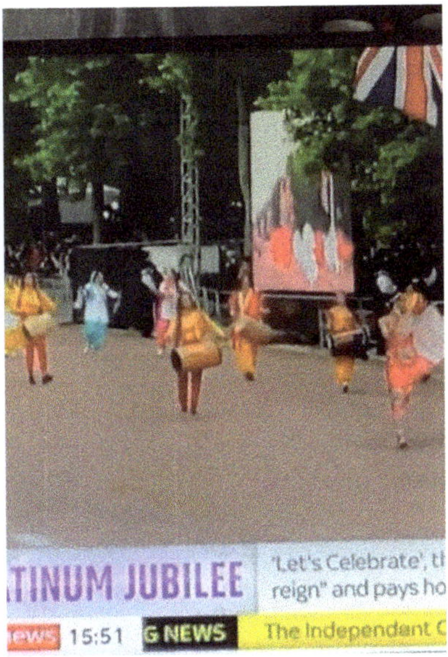
TINUM JUBILEE
15:51

Interview with Balbir Singh Bhujhangy

Song from my musical hero growing up

My musical hero was Bollywood singer Mohammed Rafi and I also looked up to Lata Mangeshkar, she is still an idol. Their music, lyrics and in-depth meaning was what inspired me throughout my life. I spent my time after school going to the Cinema to watch Bollywood movies. The nearest to our house was near the West Bromwich football ground which shut down many years ago. My favourite song of Rafi is:

First memory of a song

My first memory was when I was 7 years old. I loved listening to Yamla Jatt and Surinder Kaur who were Punjabi folk singers. My favourite songs were 'Lathe Di Chadar' by Surinder Kaur and Jamla Jatt's song, 'Sat Gur Nanak Teri Leela'.

Songs that influenced me to sing

Me and my 2 older brothers used to go to the local village festivals (Melas) and see Panjabi folk singers. There were no live bands in them times but they all used to play the traditional instruments like Tumbi (small string instrument) and Alghoza (Woodwind instrument). The songs that I remember that really made me want to sing are songs like Dulla Bhatti, Puran Bhagat, Heer Di Kali which are all famous Punjabi folks songs. This is what really pushed me to pursue my dream in singing.

Memory of songs when learning how to sing

When I moved to the UK, I started to get classical lessons from my master, Darshan Singh Bhogal and Gurdial Singh Rasiya. My mother supported me 100% and knew I really enjoyed it. The songs I got taught were classical Raag's (Poems) such as Yaman, Kaliyan and many more. I worked hard and rehearsed every day.

First song I wrote

As my family came from India, we were very poor. However, it did stop me from singing or listening to music. I started recording songs based on the struggles of people's lives, including my own. I worked in a foundry warehouse job and it involved moving and transporting sandbags to molders. I used to fill sand into a wheelbarrow for 9 hours a day which was heavy and wet, it was such a hard job to do. I created a song based on my struggles in 1966 called 'Maithon Bara Thakya Na Jawe'. A song that related to my hard work and struggles but I wrote many songs relating to my experiences in India, wedding songs and classical poems.

First song I recorded with my band

Our first recording was "Teri Chithi Noon Parthan", meaning Reading your letter. It was a very beautiful song and touched many hearts, especially those who were still waiting for their families to come to the UK or knew they would not see them for a very long time. We travelled to Uxbridge studio's to record this 4-track album with producers Sukhi and Gurnam in 1968. We recorded Live and made 100 copies of this 7" EP and then distributed the EP to all pubs with juke boxes around the Midlands. Very quickly, we became known in the community and the Bhujhangy Group name started to become famous. Many fans wanted to hear us and perform Live at their weddings, functions or Gurdwara events. We then gave this EP to Oriental Star Agencies to release our EP on their label who released our first recorded album in late 1968.

First song I performed with my band on TV

In 1969 there used to be a TV program called Friends and Neighbours, a channel which broadcasted various cultural events within the UK. We performed for the first time for Guru Nanak's Dev Ji's 500th Birthday at Smethwick Sikh temple which was broadcasted Live across the UK.

A song from your hit album

The most hit song and the most famous song from Bhujhangy Group was 'Bhabiye Akh Largayee'. This was a real hit in the 1970's and is still playing at weddings today. This song even featured in the BBC Asian Network's top 50 Bhangra songs of all time.

A song connected to a happy moment with my band

In those days, we had no telephones, no TV, no social media but a lot of friends to socialize with in the evenings. Every Friday and most evenings after a long day at work, all our friends used to meet up and bring bottles of beer, whisky, brandy and vodka and we would sing, dance and drink. I wrote a song with the band called 'Waleyti Peeni aan' which means I want to drink an English drink. A very popular song released in 1969 and still played now at weddings. This song also featured in the BBC Asian Networks all-time top 50 Bhangra songs. A huge song, enjoyed by the lads, we had great memories performing this song at weddings.

A song from a competition

There were many Asian Song Contests held yearly from 1975 to 1980, I took part in them every year. In 1977, the contest was held at the Wembley Conference Hall now called Wembley Arena in London. The competition was to sing Urdu Ghazal's (Poem's) where there were many competing international artists and bands. This was a great memory as we were runners up for this competition. A great moment for me and my band Bhujhangy as it was an international competition.

Song from my wedding day

Bhujhangy Group members at the time sang at my wedding and they sang a special Sehra (Poem) which linked all my family members together along with all the cities they all came from. They sang many songs that day and I still have my wedding movie somewhere, it was rare at the time but women in my family attended the party.

Favorite song from a Genre of music

It's been 55 years since I have been singing on stage and I have recorded over 300 songs as a vocalist with my brother Dalbir.
A mixture of the below:
Religious songs (Shabads)
Bhangra Songs
Punjabi and Urdu Poems (Ghazals)
Special Wedding Songs (Sara Sikhiya)
Hindi songs

My favourite genre of music has to be singing Bhangra songs. We mixed traditional Punjabi instruments like Tumbi (string), Dhol (Big drum) with Guitar and Drumkit, creating a unique sound which was very fresh in the late 60's. We were the first Bhangra band to record a Punjabi folk song in the UK.

A song connected to a sad moment of your life

Mohammed Rafi's 'Baabul Ki Duayen Leti Ja' is a sad song about daughter's getting married and leaving their family home. I have two daughters, both of which are married and that song reminds me of my daughters.

Memory of a song from your musical journey

Being the first Bhangra group to start Bhangra music in the UK, our popularity was growing day by day. Our performances in the local temples and pubs from the Midlands turned into performances across the UK. One famous song I sung on all these performances was called Ik Pal meaning stay a little while. In this song I used to mention all the cities I performed in and linked the audience into the lyrics. Very popular amongst the crowds who were great fans of Bhujhangy.

What was the best time of your life?

The best time of my life was the time my mother was alive. After her death, I struggled and missed her so much and life became a lot harder.

The most important bit of information you want to pass on to your children.

Whatever you want to do in life, you should go for it, as life is too short. You should never get too sad or too happy, try and stay in control and carry on with life as positively as you can. Also never forget the friends who helped you during a difficult time.

What is your secret to happiness and living a good life?

I remained in God's will and kept away from the bad things in life. I stopped drinking alcohol and stopped eating meat in

1979 when my mother died. It changed my life and taught me nothing is forever...

What would you like to see future generations accomplish?

I'd advise them to stick to their culture and music. To learn history, especially based around Sikhs, and most importantly, stick together with you families and help them as much as you can.

Who would you like to thank?

I respect all artists as my little brothers and children. I would like to thank all radio, TV programs, gurdwaras, newspapers, family, friends, fans and people of the world who have kept bhangra alive and appreciated my singing. Because of the public's support, I have reached 55 years of singing.

I would like to thank almighty God because without his grace I could not cope with life's ups and downs, he has helped me every time and everywhere. I wish for my kids and grandchildren to pray to God; he will help you in every way.

Any words of wisdom?

Everybody must die one day, we must be good human beings and stay strong, we should leave with good memories and hope to be remembered by people positively.

Life is short, enjoy your life, achieve your goals, don't wait for happiness, make happiness for yourself.

Don't get too happy and don't feel too sad, stay neutral and ride the waves of life.

Visit: www.bhujhangy.co.uk
https://www.facebook.com/balbirbhujhangy.singh/about
https://twitter.com/BhujhangyGroup

www.ingramcontent.com/pod-product-compliance
Lightning Source LLC
LaVergne TN
LVHW010305070426
835508LV00026B/3436
* 9 7 8 1 8 0 3 8 1 1 9 6 3 *